Ms. Albin Meets Jackson Pollack

Written and Illustrated by Kelli Albin

Dedication:

To all of my artsy friends. You know who you are...

ACKNOWLEDGEMENTS

Thank you to everyone that helped with this book.

PREVIOUS BOOKS BY KELLI ALBIN

Ms. Albin Rides the Bus

Ms. Albin Takes a Vacation

"Atticuss, what would you like to do today?" asked Ms. Albin.

"Visit a museum? What a wonderful idea! Let's go!"

Ms. Albin packed the cats, Sadi and Atticuss, into their carrier, buckled them into the car, and away they went to visit the art museum.

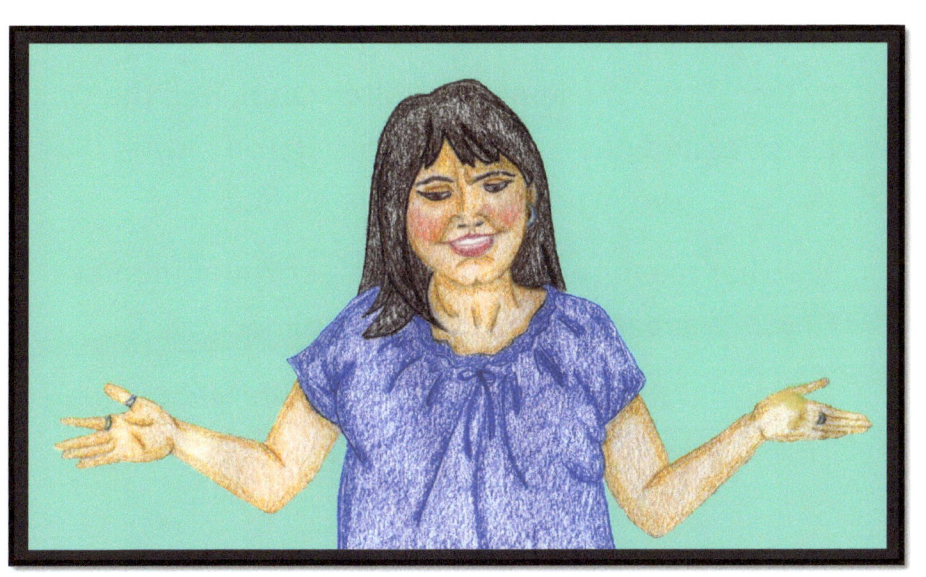

Once at the museum, Ms. Albin cautioned the cats to be quiet and not touch the paintings on display. She gave Atticuss a meaningful look.

"That means no licking, Atticuss! You remember what happened the last time."

Sadi did the eye roll as she remembered the loud alarms, frantic museum guards, and the police sirens...

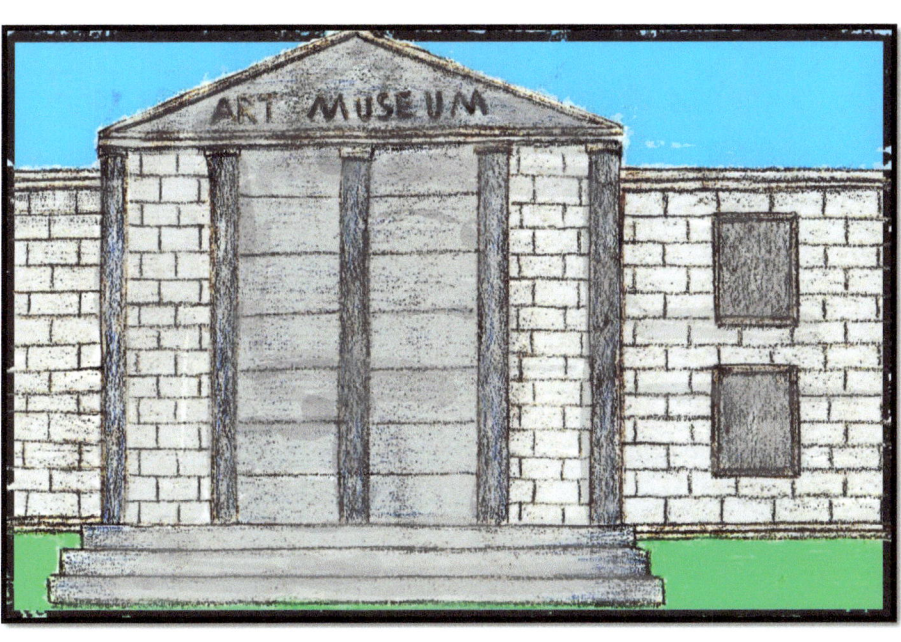

Inside they oohed over the Van Gogh's, aahed over the O'Keefe's, and sighed over the Monet's. Then they came to an unusual piece, a Jackson Pollock painting. They stopped and looked, but didn't say anything. They didn't really know what to say. Atticuss loved the colors and "action" in the painting. Sadi thought it stunk.

"Big deal. I can do that." she thought.

Ms. Albin was interested in the texture and vibrancy in the painting.

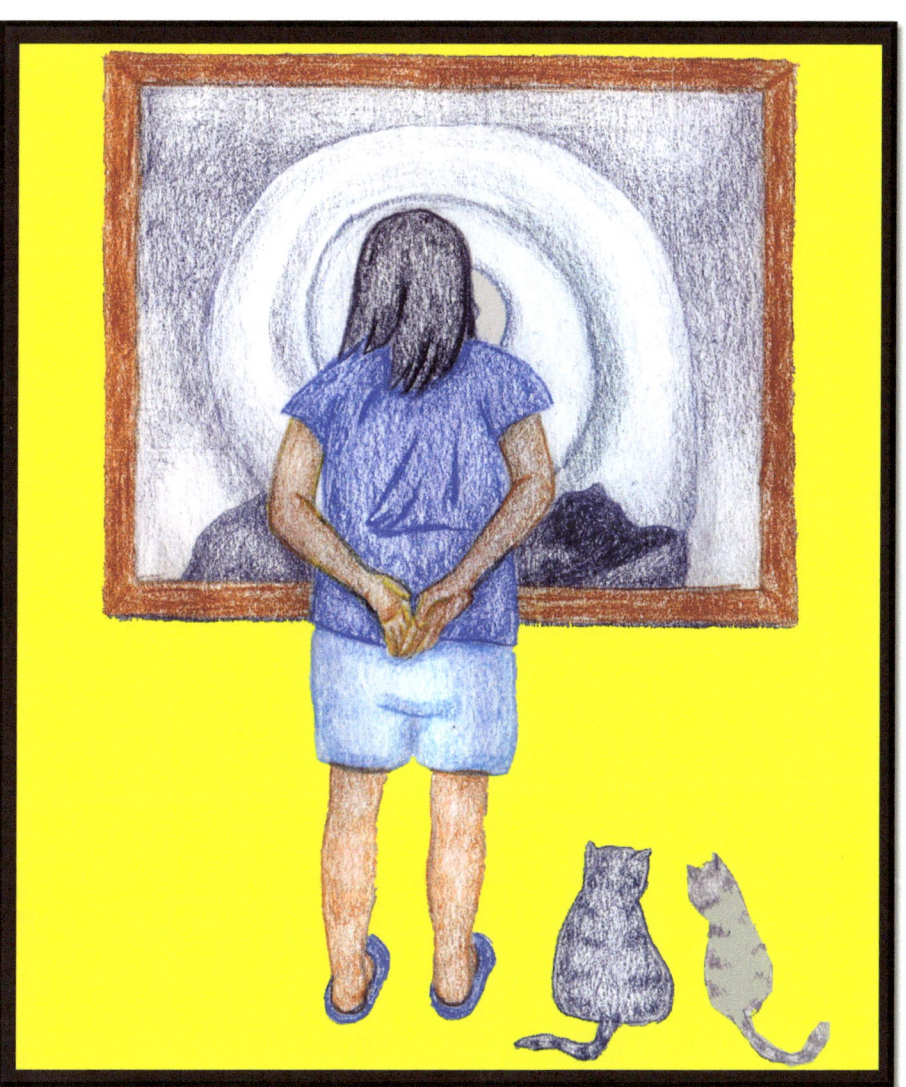

Being the art teacher that she is, she couldn't help explaining to the cats that Pollock created his paintings by laying the canvas on the floor and dripping the paint on it. It's the kind of art that anyone can do. It doesn't necessarily take talent or skill, but it does take a good eye for balance and design. If there is too much paint on one area of the painting you can create balance by adding a bright color to draw the eye to another area of the painting.

"The texture of the paint makes you want to reach out and touch it doesn't it?" she asked.

"Don't even think about it, Atticuss!" she warned.

She went on to explain that this kind of painting is called "action painting", a form of abstract art. The jumble of splashes, lines, and splotches create a sense of movement.

"Almost like it is alive!" Ms. Albin exclaimed.

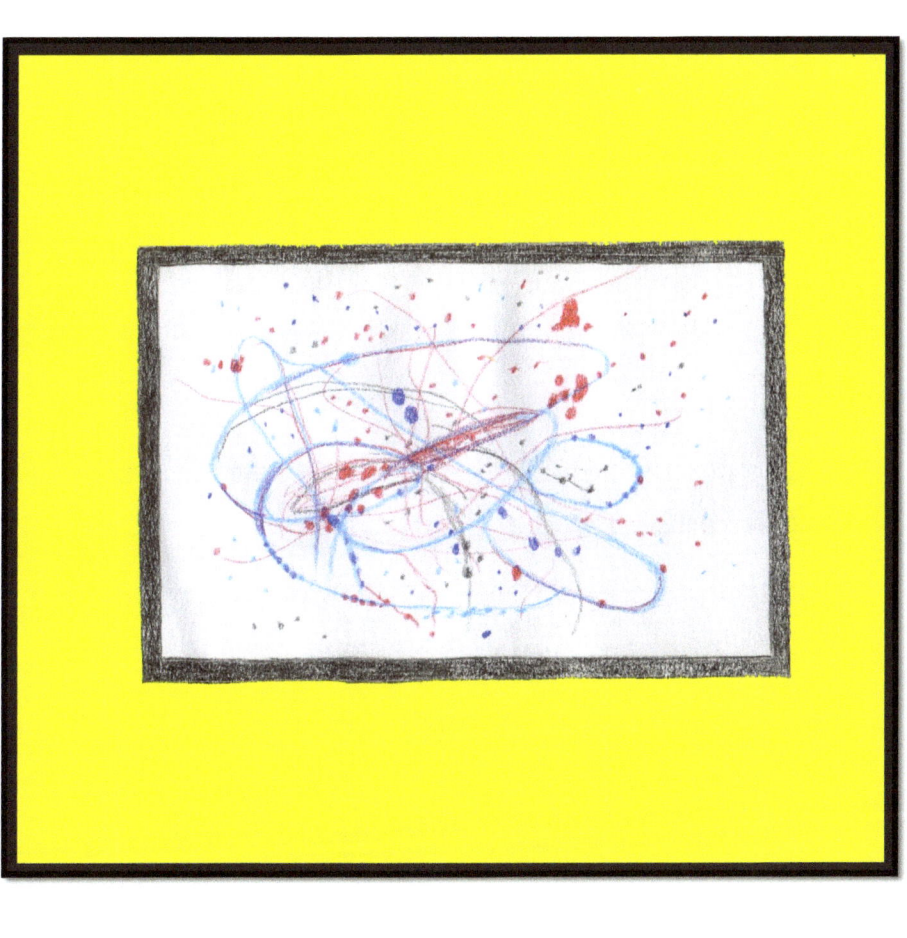

As she studied the painting she became lost in thought...suddenly Jackson Pollock walked into the room.

"How do you like my masterpieces?" he asked.

Before any of them could answer, he exclaimed that what he liked best about his art is that it is controversial.

"You either love it or you hate it! Nobody can look at it and not have an opinion. You have to get involved!"

"So true." thought Ms. Albin.

"Hey kids." Pollock shouted "Want to have some fun? Help me with my painting!"

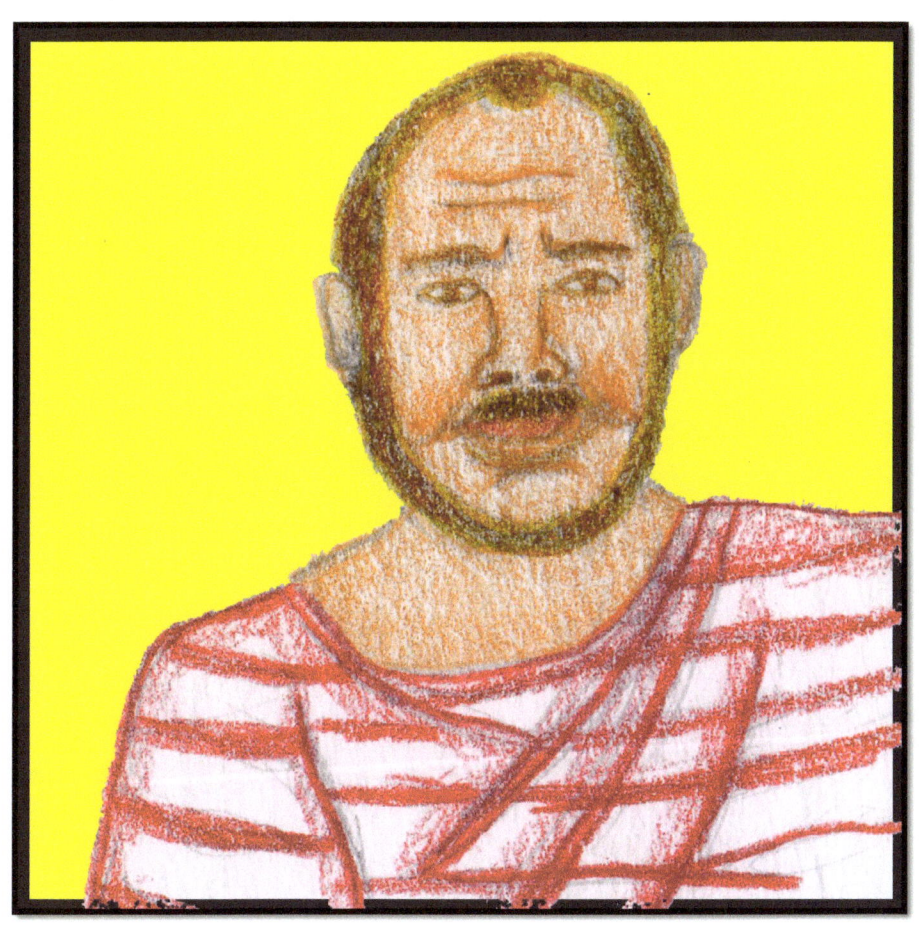

With a flourish he gave each cat a bucket of paint and some brushes. They began to splash paint on the canvas that immediately appeared on the floor. It didn't take long before the paint began to fly all over each other, as well as the painting.

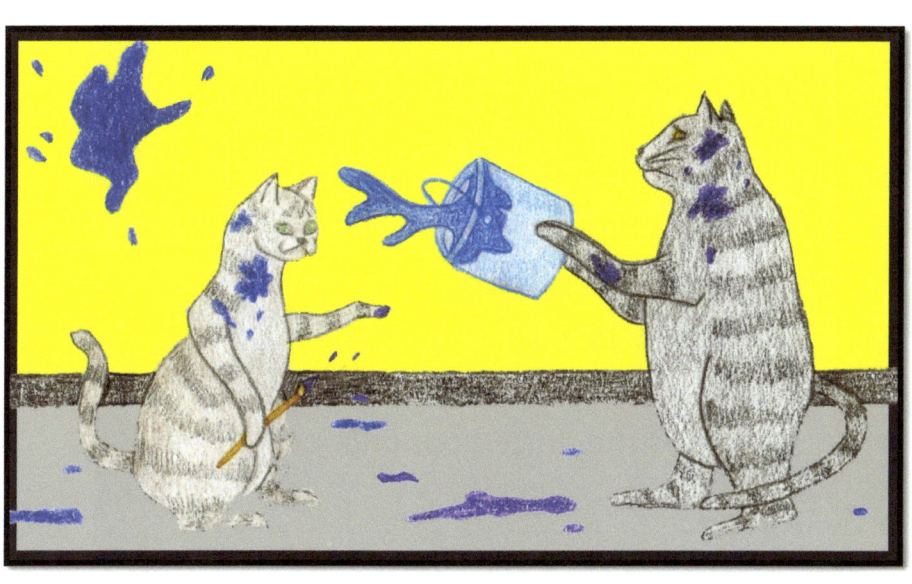

When they were through, the cats sprawled exhausted, in the middle of the canvas. They looked like they were a part of the painting itself. Pollock was ecstatic. He wanted to keep the cats on permanent display, but Ms. Albin vetoed that idea. Nervously, she quickly hustled the cats out of the room….Ms. Albin gave herself a little shake as she drifted out of her daydream.

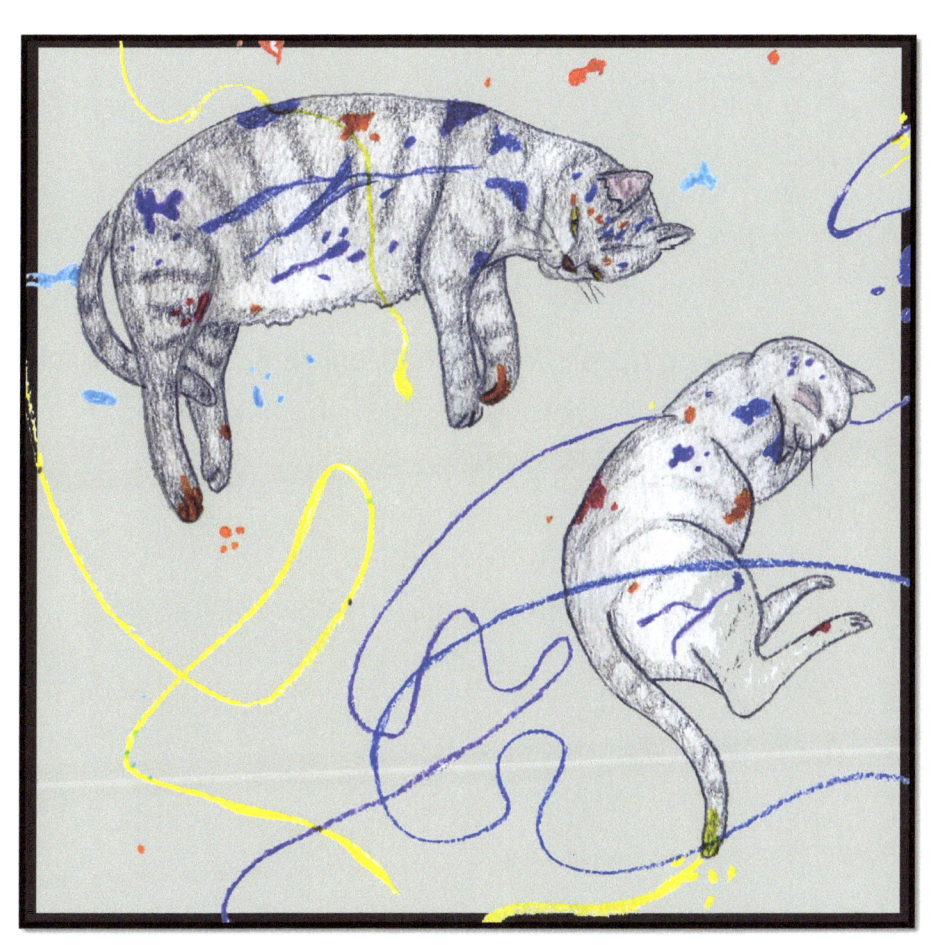

"Let's go kids" she said, as she gathered up her brood.

"Time to go home. We've had enough adventure for today. Is anyone hungry?" she asked.

Two pair of paws went up into the air.

"Typical," thought Ms. Albin...but they were all smiling as they left the museum and went home for lunch.

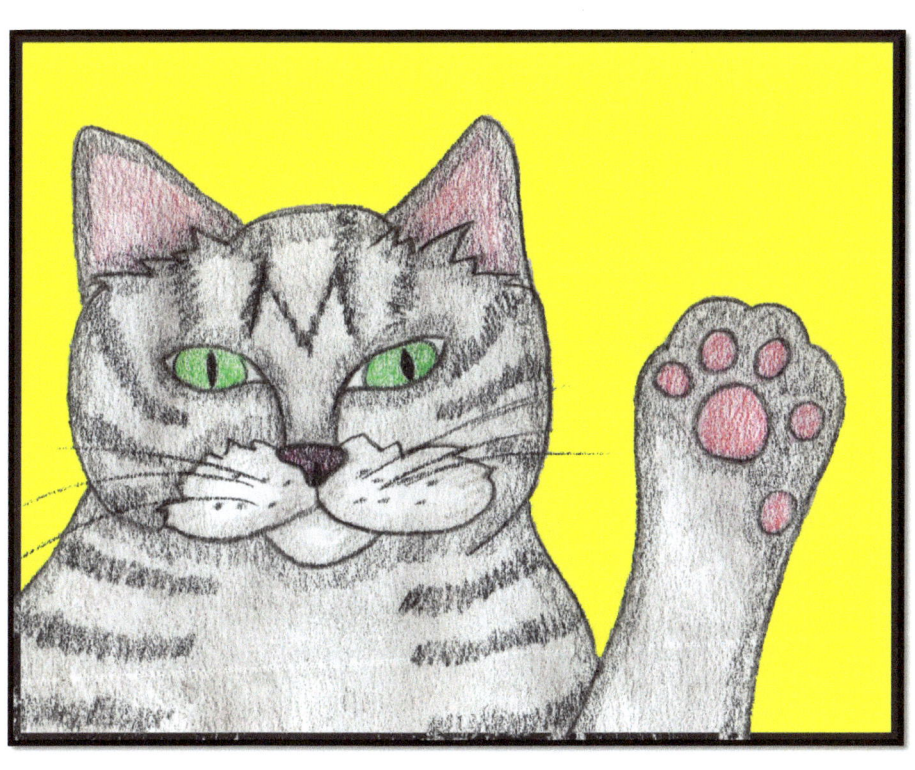

ABOUT THE AUTHOR

Kelli Albin earned her commercial art degree from Oral Roberts University and her certifications of art and reading from Missouri State University. She also completed her masters at MSU. She is currently teaching art, K-12, at Dora School, and she teaches photography at MSU. She lives with her feline child, Atticuss, and pursues her interests of art, photography, and reading.